The Little Book of BIG FEELINGS

Calming My ANXIETY

The Little Book of BIG FEELINGS

Calming My ANXIETY

Copyright © 2024 by KLB Bookworks LLC - All rights reserved.

The content contained within this book may not be reproduced, duplicated or transmitted without direct written permission from the author or the publisher.

Under no circumstances will any blame or legal responsibility be held against the publisher, or author, for any damages, reparation, or monetary loss due to the information contained within this book. Either directly or indirectly. You are responsible for your own choices, actions, and results.

Legal Notice:

This book is copyright protected. This book is only for personal use. You cannot amend, distribute, sell, use, quote or paraphrase any part, or the content within this book, without the consent of the author or publisher.

Disclaimer Notice:

Please note the information contained within this document is for educational and entertainment purposes only. All effort has been executed to present accurate, up to date, and reliable, complete information. No warranties of any kind are declared or implied. Readers acknowledge that the author is not engaging in the rendering of legal, financial, medical or professional advice. The content within this book has been derived from various sources. Please consult a licensed professional before attempting any techniques outlined in this book.

By reading this document, the reader agrees that under no circumstances is the author responsible for any losses, direct or indirect, which are incurred as a result of the use of the information contained within this document, including, but not limited to, — errors, omissions, or inaccuracies.

This Book Belongs To:

....

....

The Little Book of

As a way of saying thank you.
I am thrilled to gift you this FREE coloring book.

To get instant access just scan QR code or go to:

www.booksbyluna.com

The Little Book of BIG FEELINGS

Thank You

Thank you so much for choosing "The Little Book of Big Feelings."

I know there are so many wonderful books out there, and I'm truly honored that you picked mine.

It means the world to me that you've taken this journey with me and my characters, and I hope the story has touched your heart as much as it did mine while creating it.

Before you go, I have a small favor to ask. If you enjoyed the book, would you kindly consider leaving a review on the platform? Sharing your thoughts is the best way to support authors like me, and it helps others discover the magic of stories that nurture young minds.

Your feedback is so valuable—it helps me continue crafting books that inspire and support little readers like yours. I'd love to hear from you, and it would mean everything to know how the story resonated with you and your family.

Thank you again for being part of this adventure! Your support and feedback mean the world to me.

With heartfelt thanks,

Luna Rinne

Talent Show Tomorrow.!

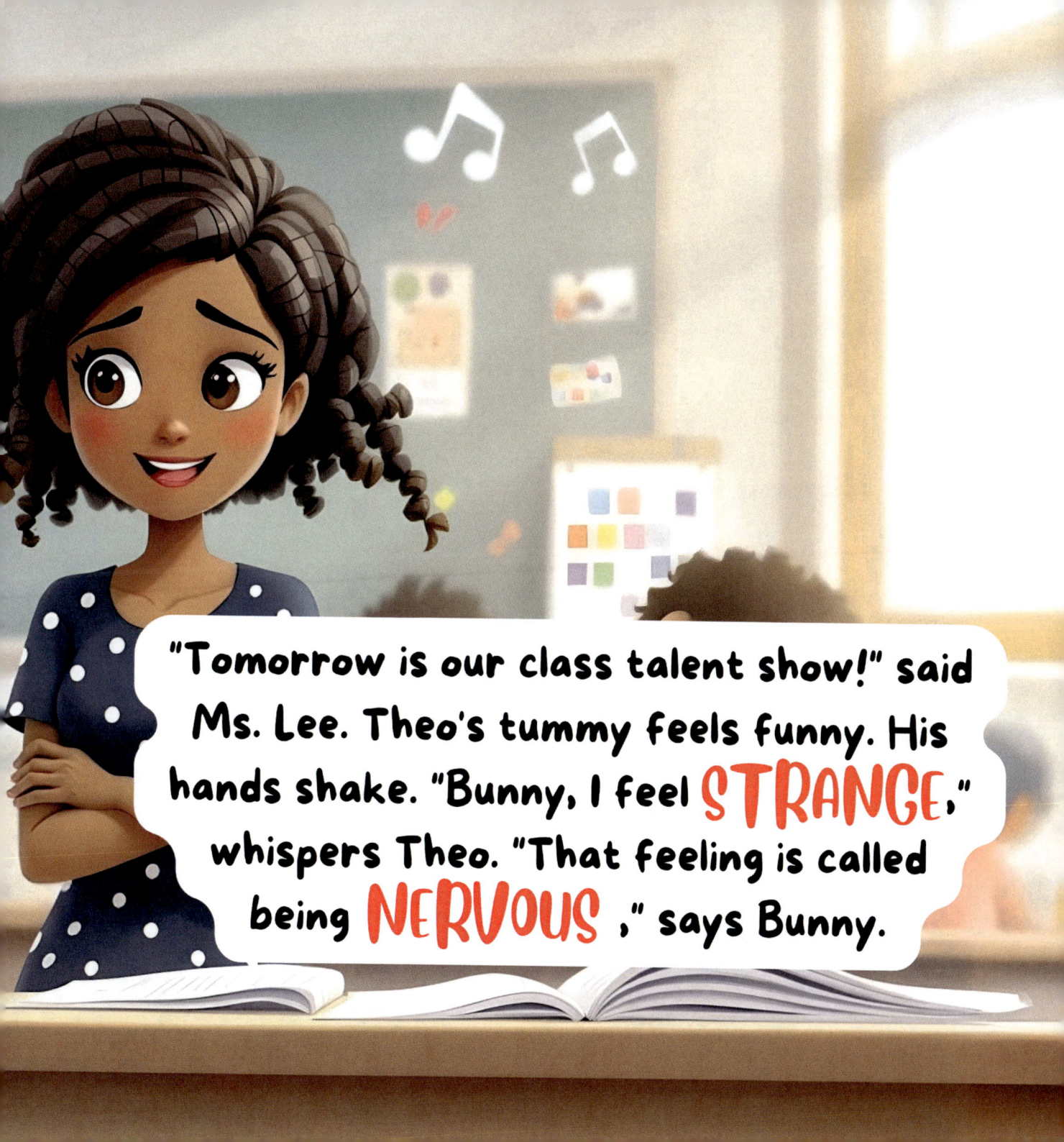

"Tomorrow is our class talent show!" said Ms. Lee. Theo's tummy feels funny. His hands shake. "Bunny, I feel **STRANGE**," whispers Theo. "That feeling is called being **NERVOUS**," says Bunny.

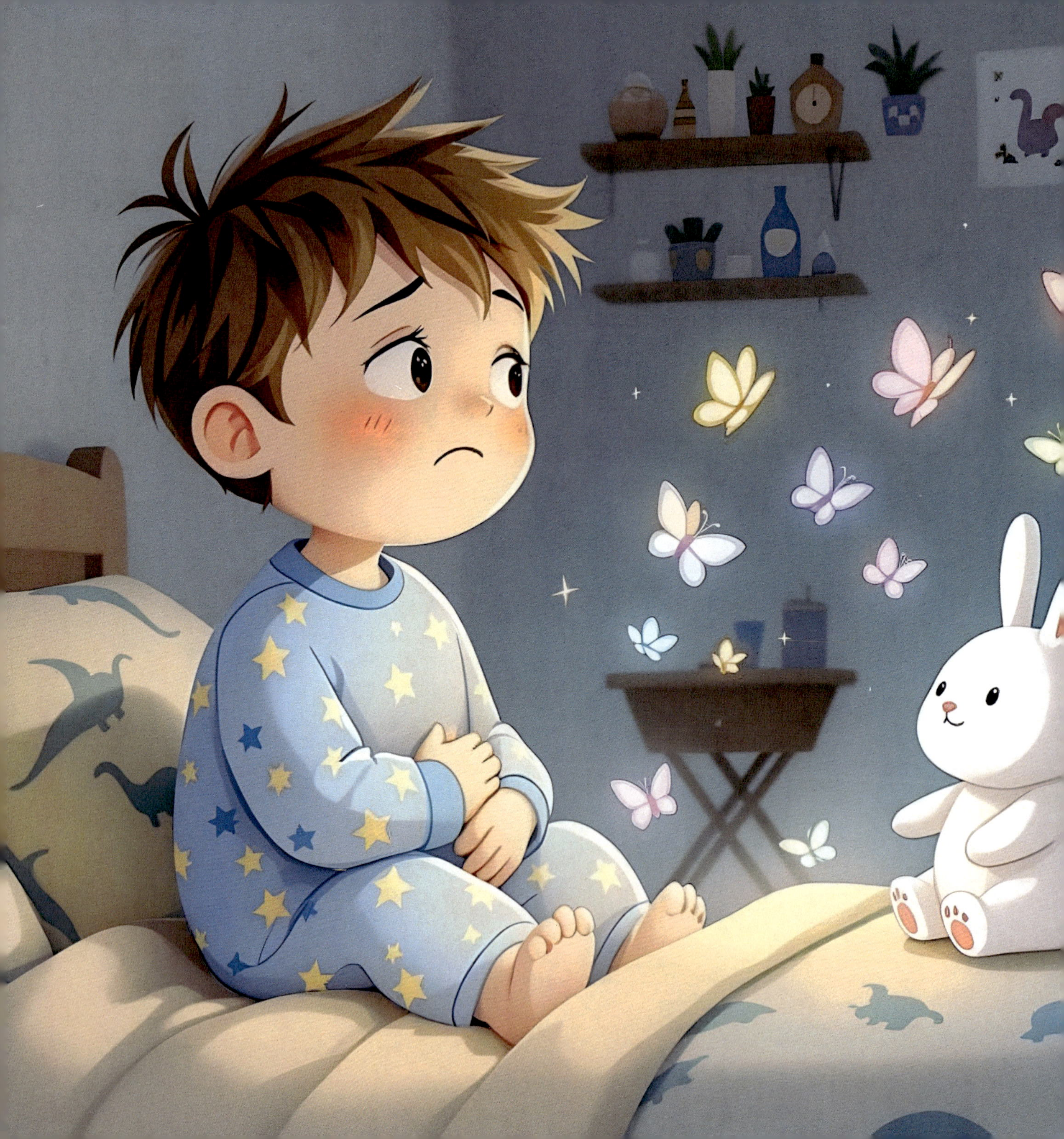

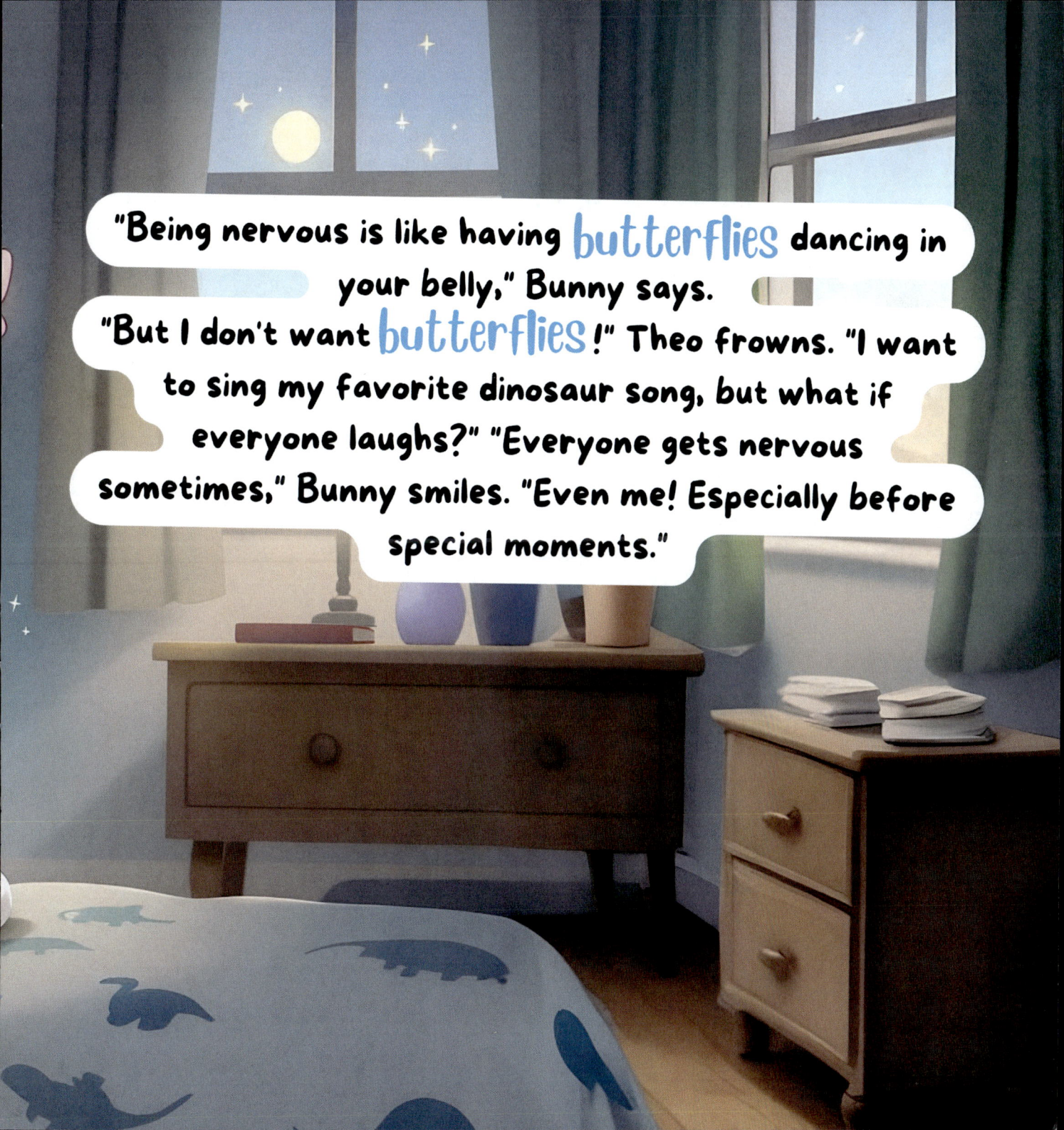

"Being nervous is like having **butterflies** dancing in your belly," Bunny says.
"But I don't want **butterflies**!" Theo frowns. "I want to sing my favorite dinosaur song, but what if everyone laughs?" "Everyone gets nervous sometimes," Bunny smiles. "Even me! Especially before special moments."

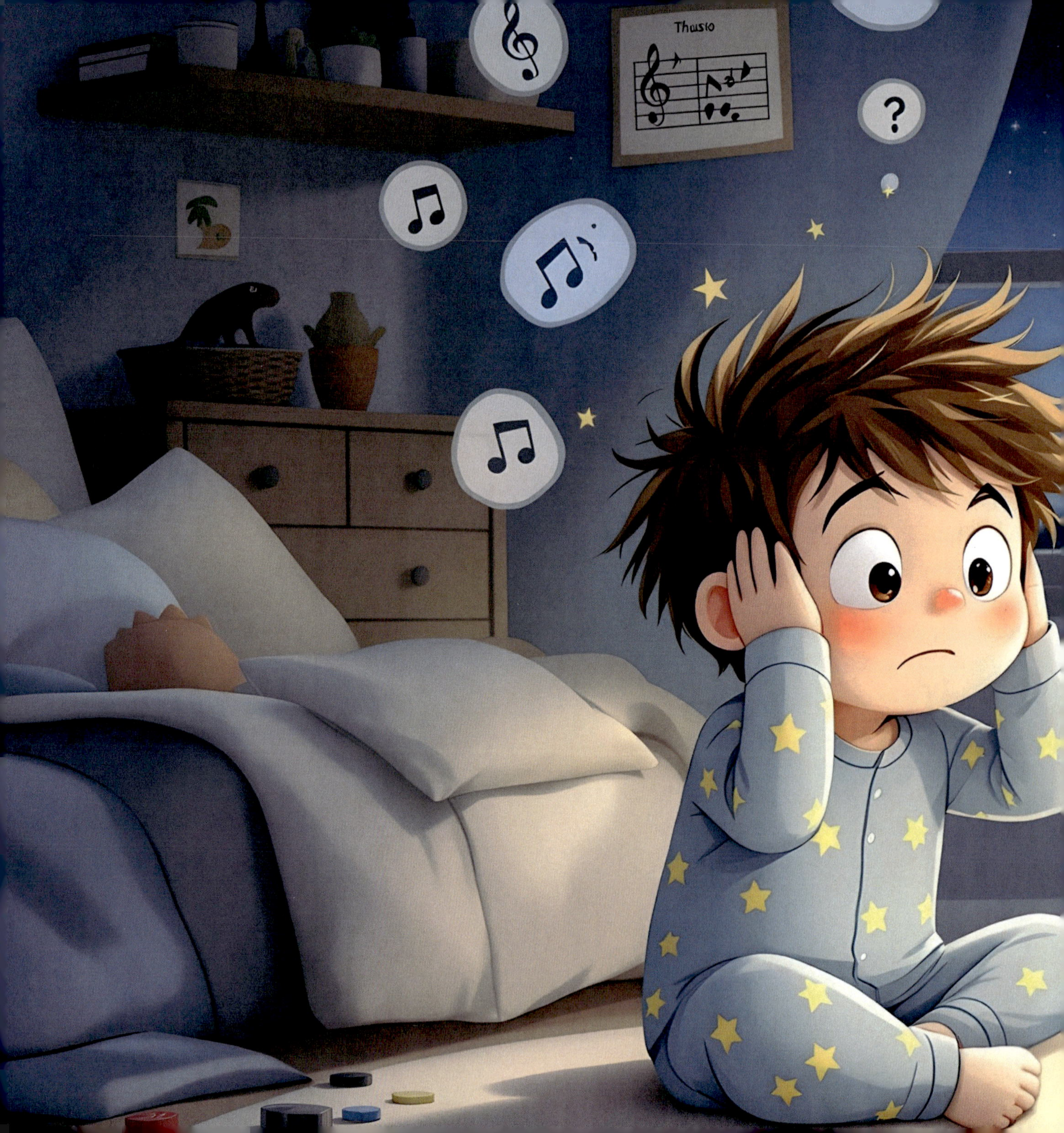
Thusio
?

"**What if** I forget the words? **What if** my voice gets squeaky?" Theo worries. "Ah," says Bunny, "your mind is playing the '**What if**' game. Let's play a different game instead!"

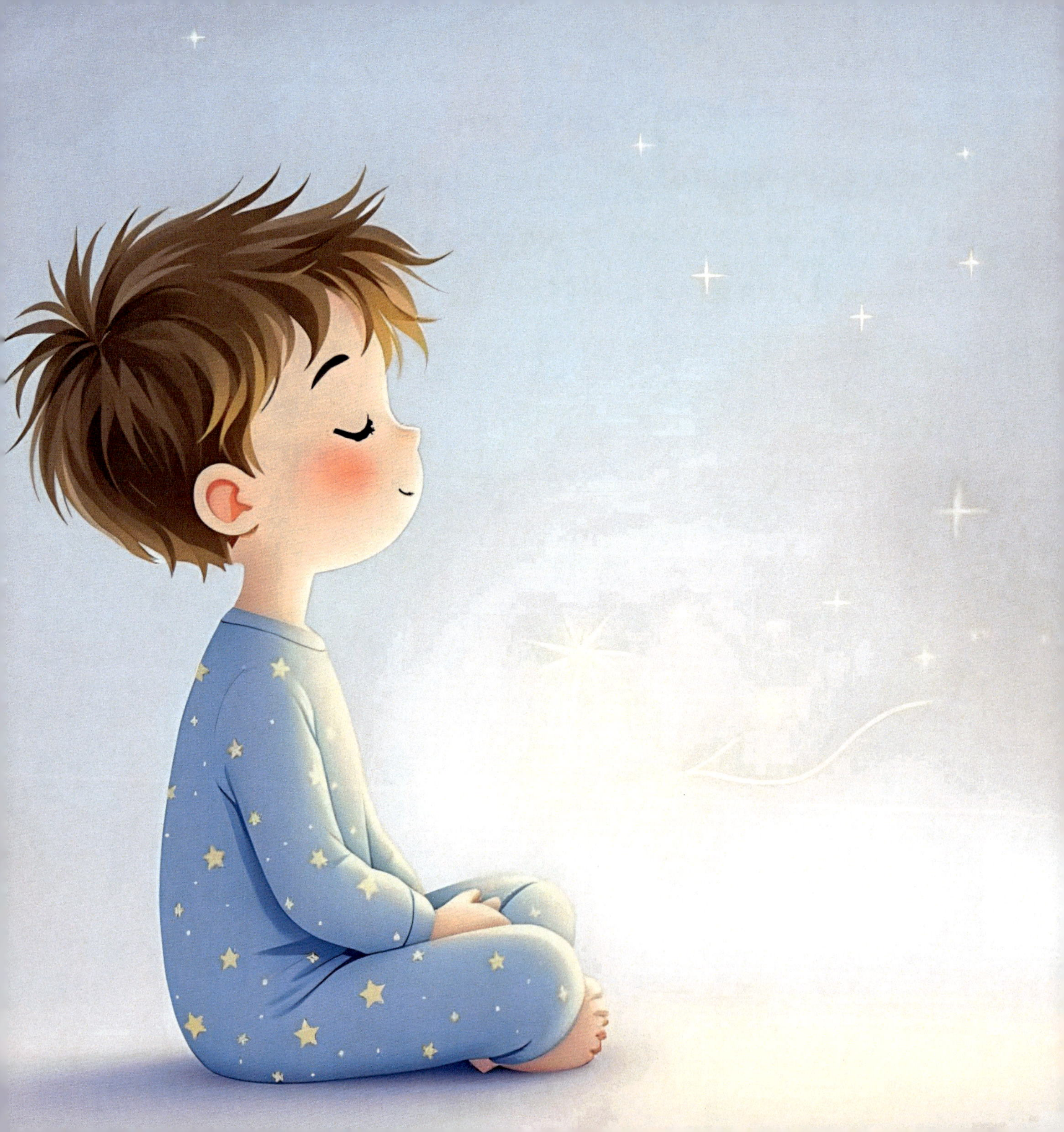

"Close your eyes," Bunny says softly. "Now take **a big breath in**, like you're smelling a flower... And blow out slowly, like you're making a **dandelion** dance."

"Let's do it *again*," says Bunny.
"Smell the flower... blow the dandelion..."
Theo's shoulders feel soft now.
"*Good Job!*" says Bunny.

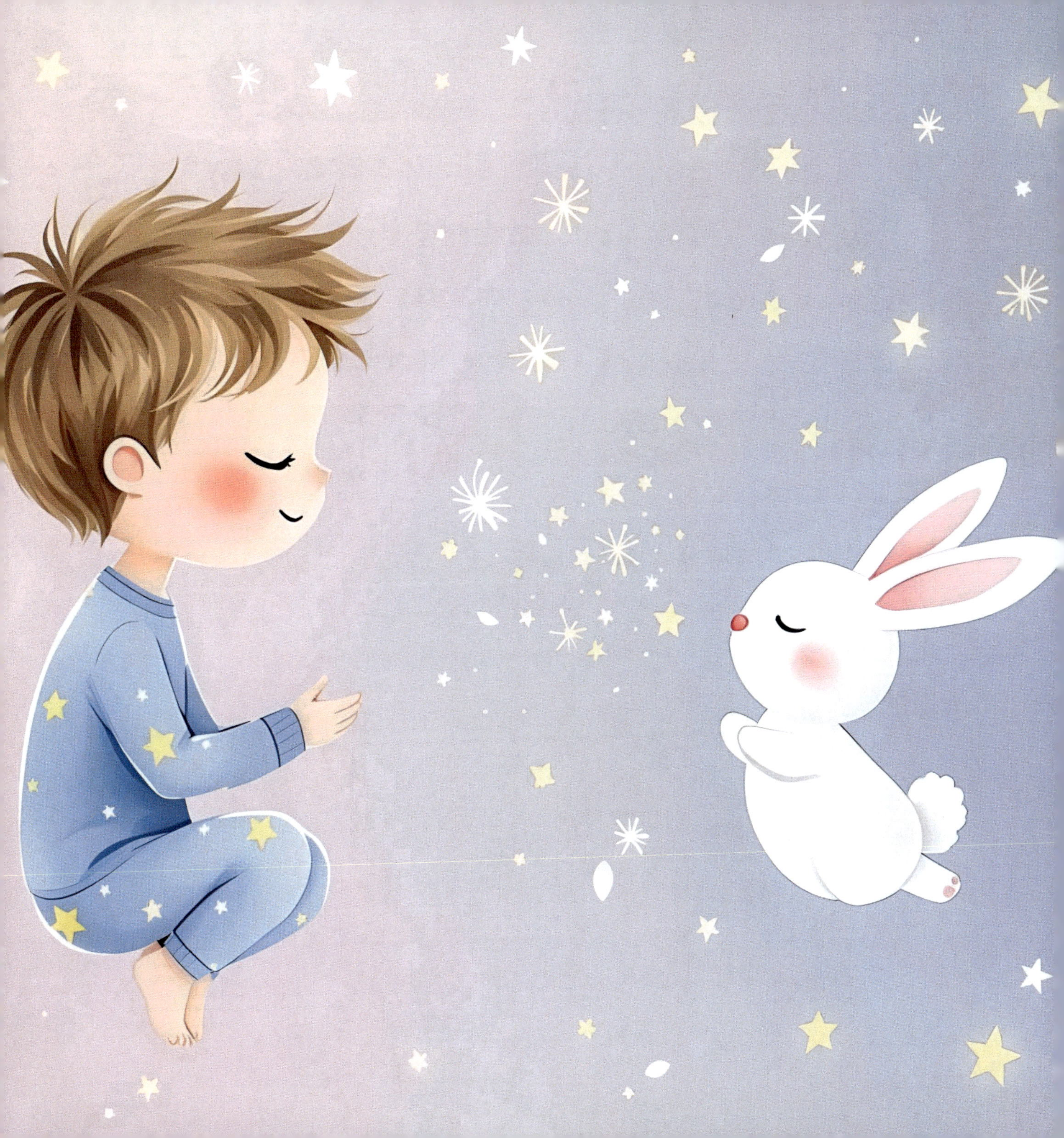

"Let's SING your song here," says Bunny. "Just you and me by this tree." Theo sings his song about T-Rex. He knows all the words!

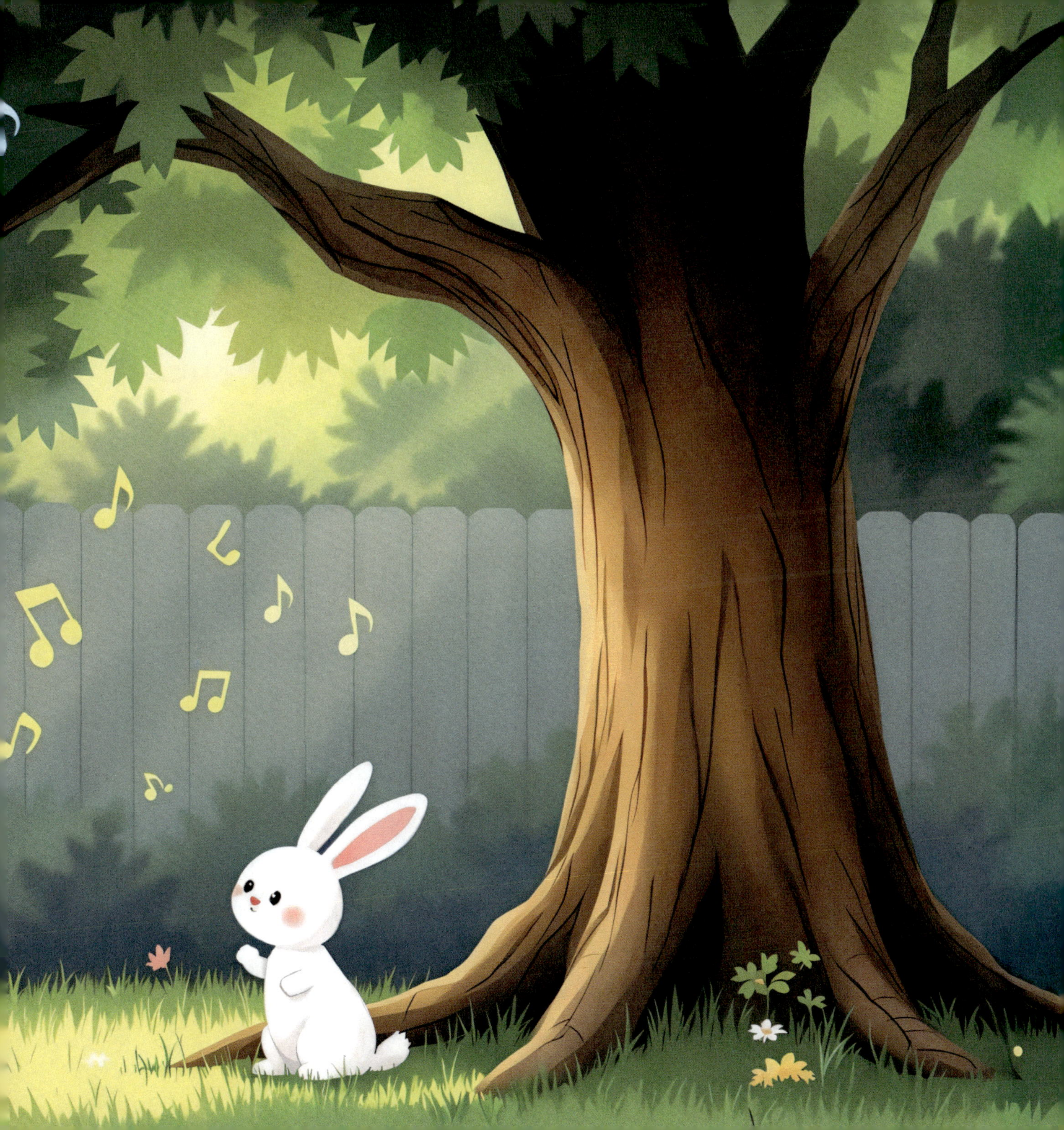

"What if others SING better than me?" asks Theo. "The show is not about being the best," says Bunny. "It's about having fun! And you LOVE dinosaurs!"

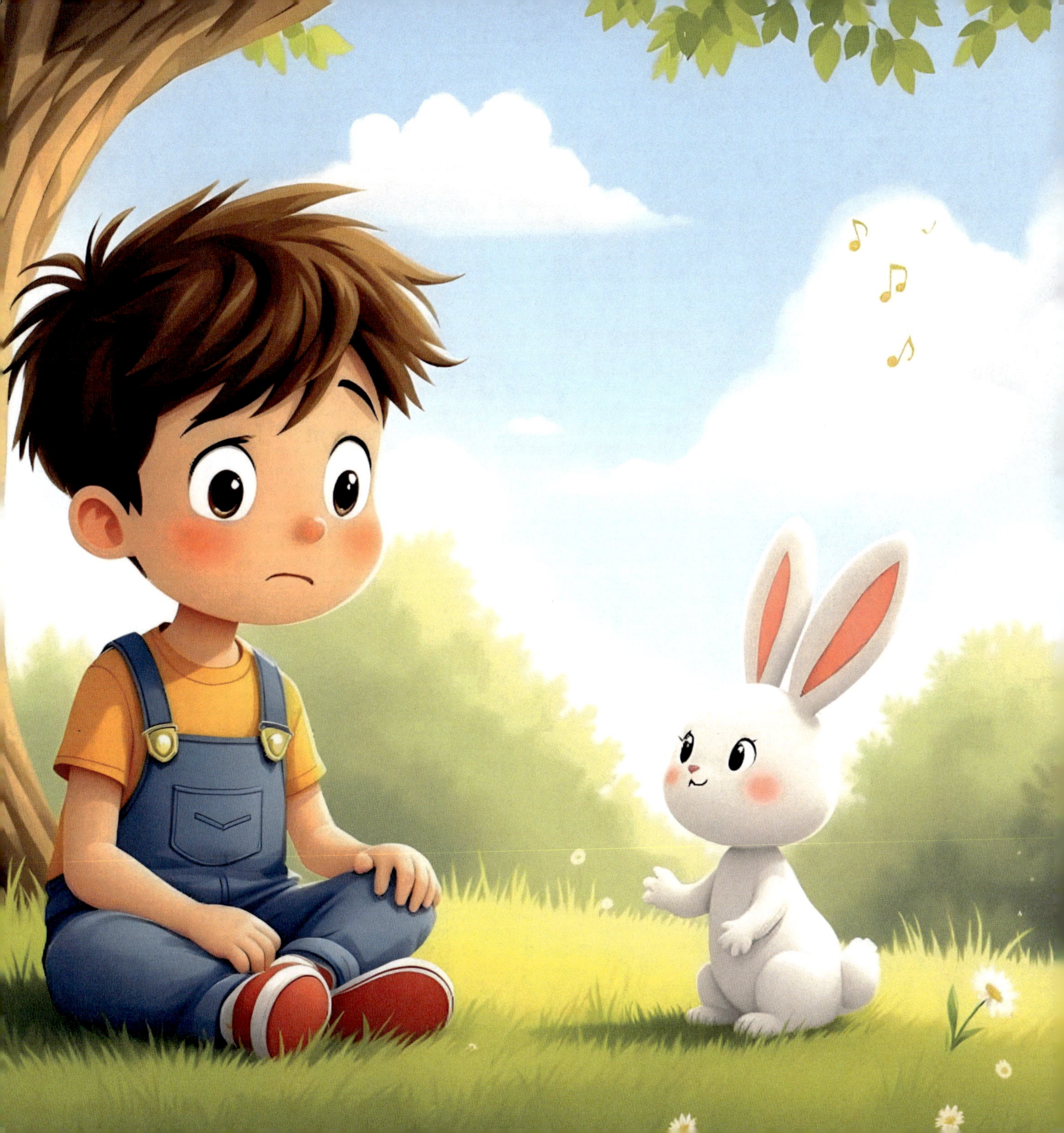

"Remember when you were scared to **ROAR** for baby sister?" asks Bunny. "Now she **LOVES** your roars! Sometimes scary things become fun things."

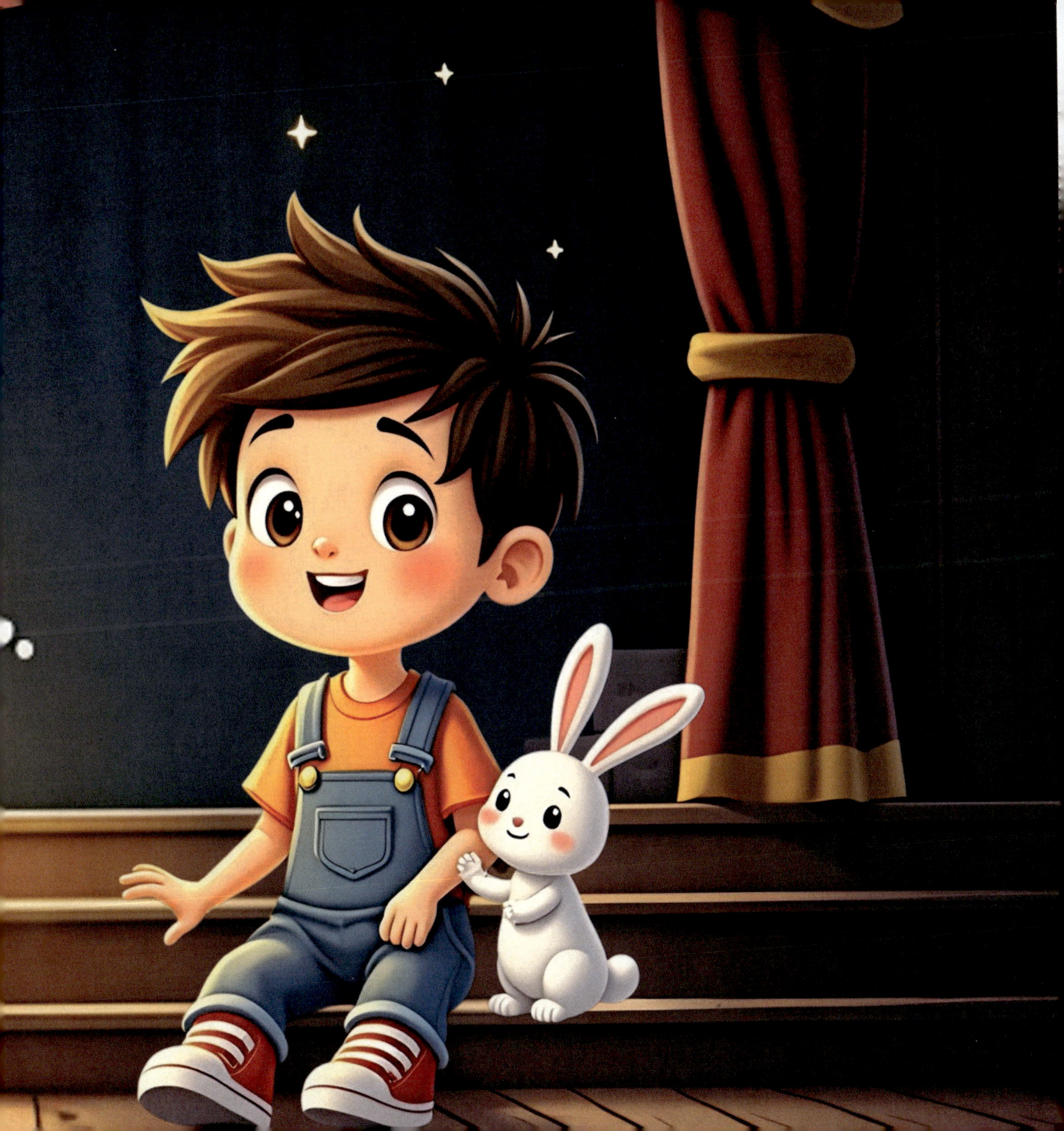

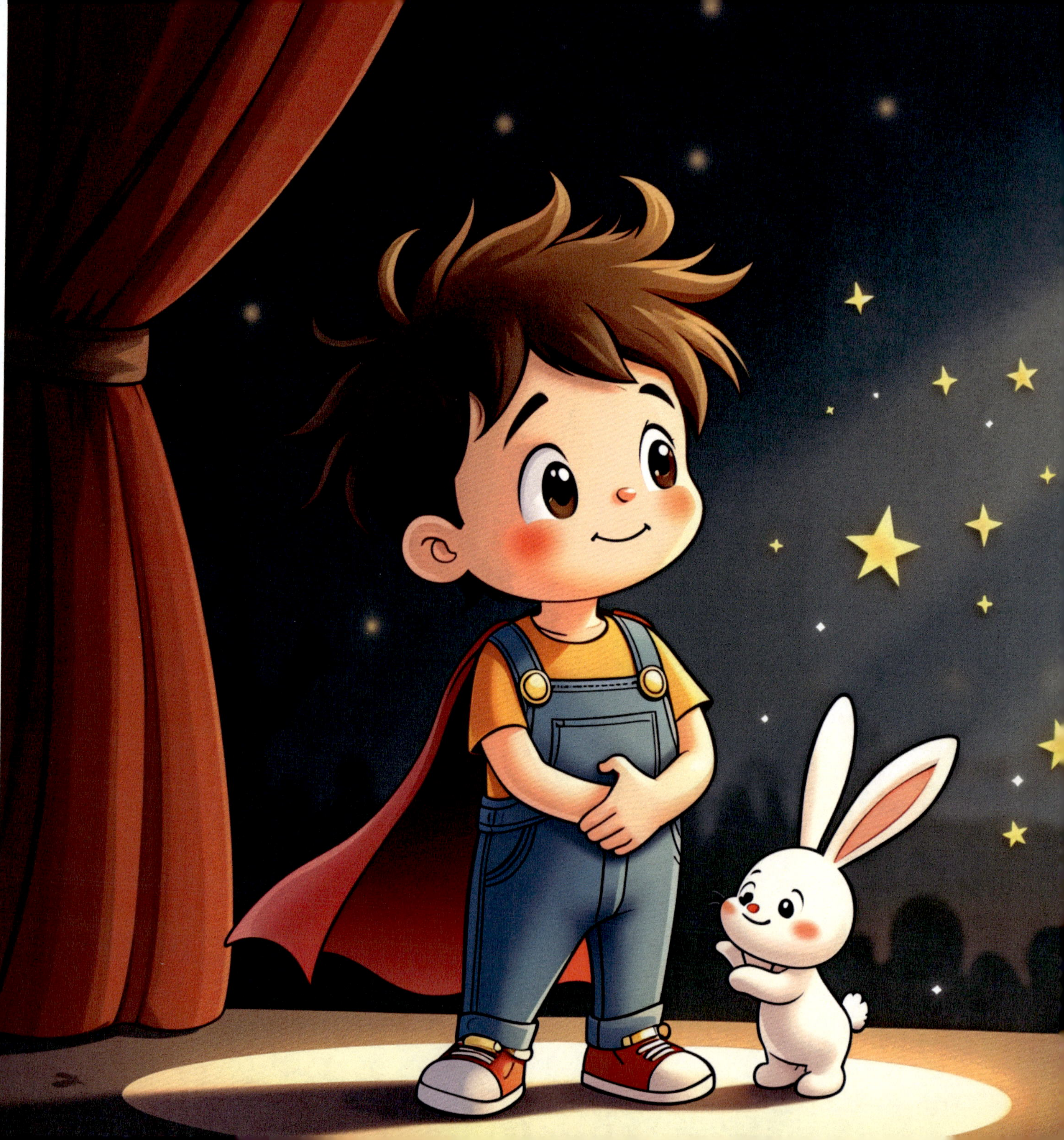

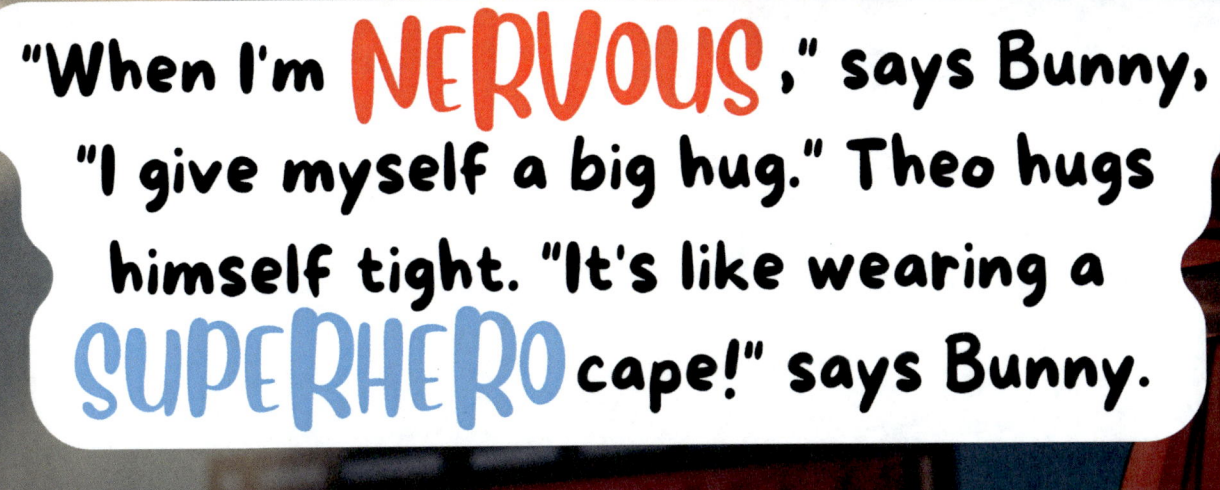

"When I'm NERVOUS," says Bunny, "I give myself a big hug." Theo hugs himself tight. "It's like wearing a SUPERHERO cape!" says Bunny.

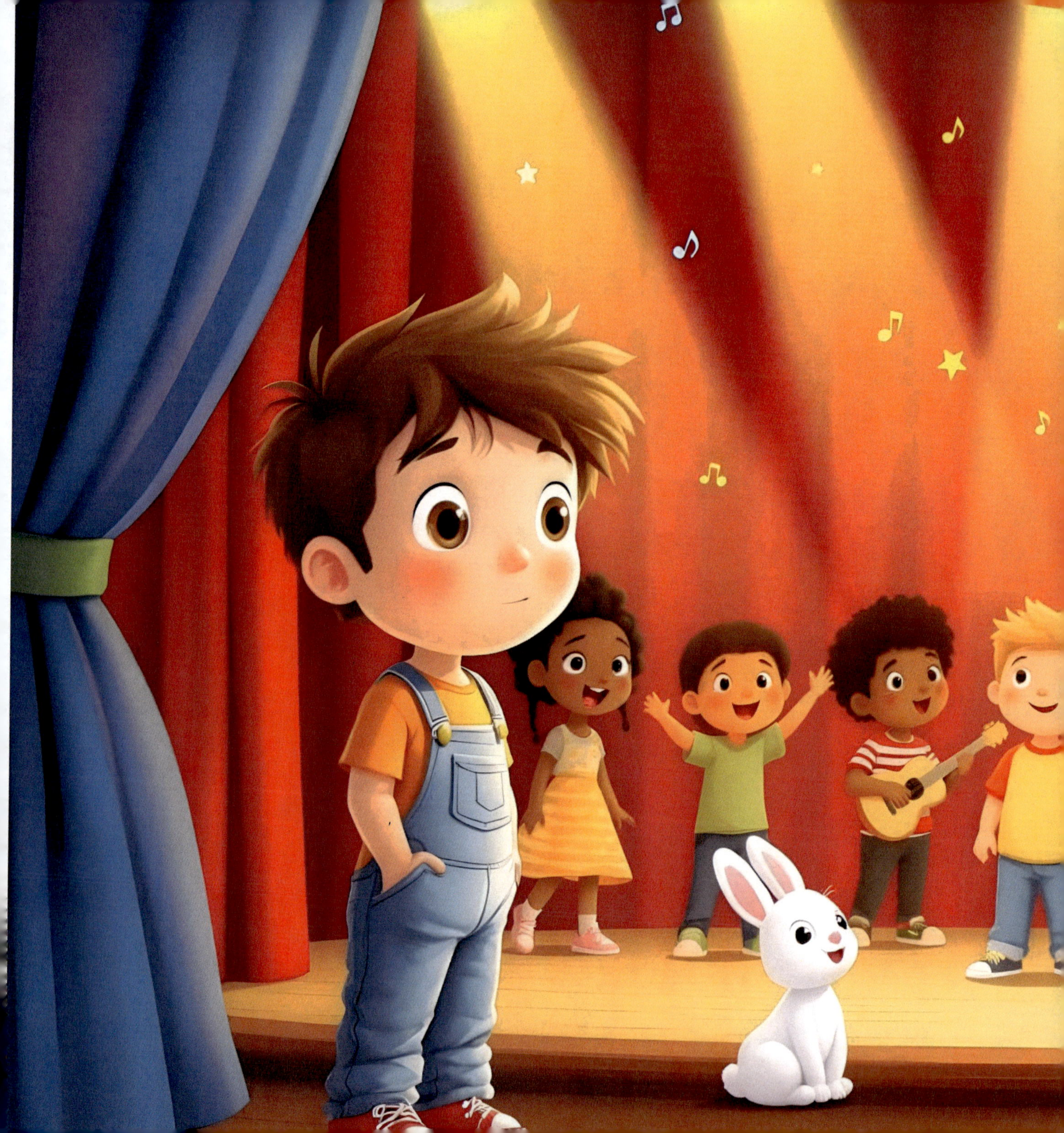

"I have an IDEA," says Bunny. "I'll stay in your pocket. When you need me, just pat your pocket!"

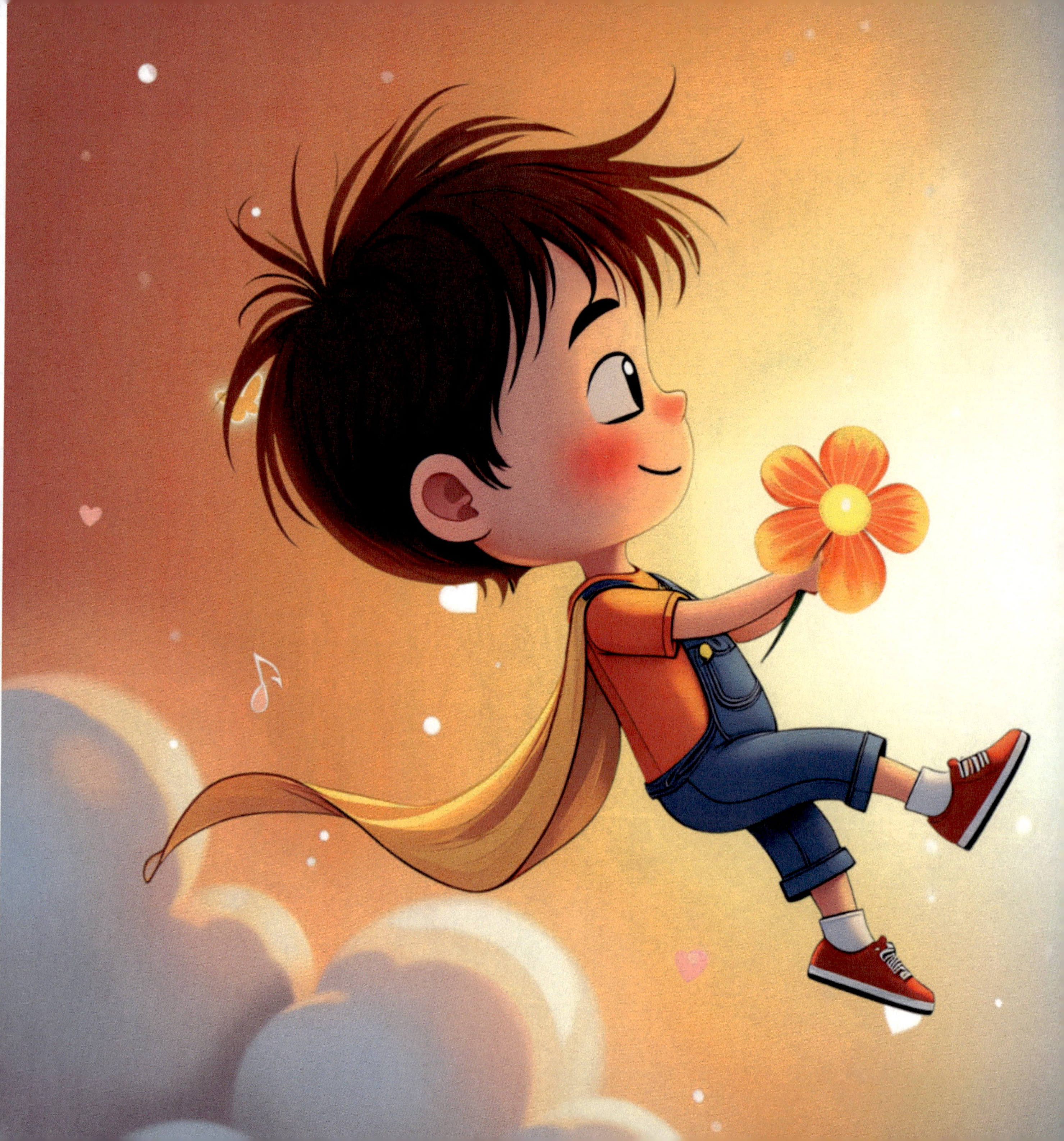

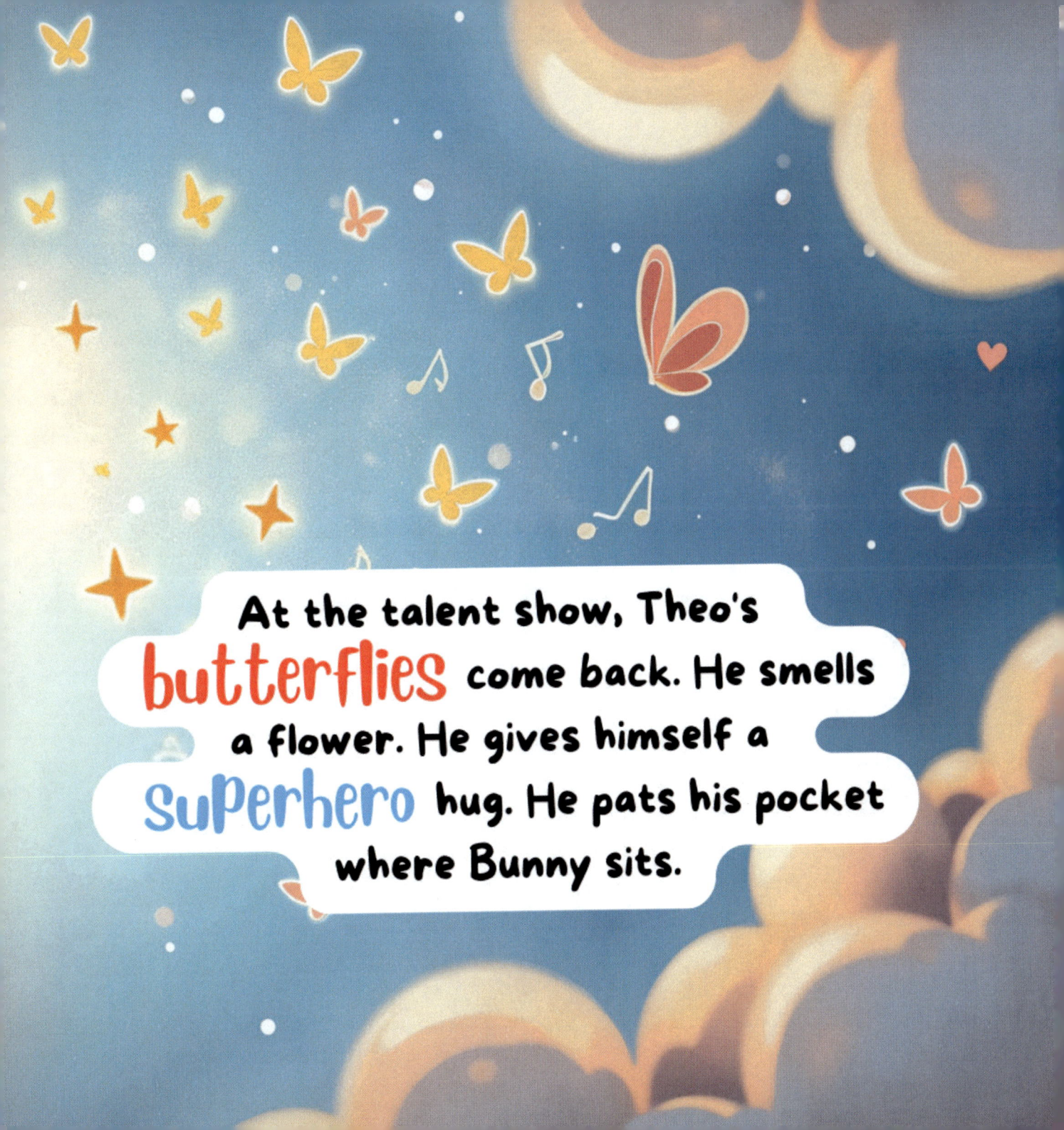

At the talent show, Theo's **butterflies** come back. He smells a flower. He gives himself a **superhero** hug. He pats his pocket where Bunny sits.

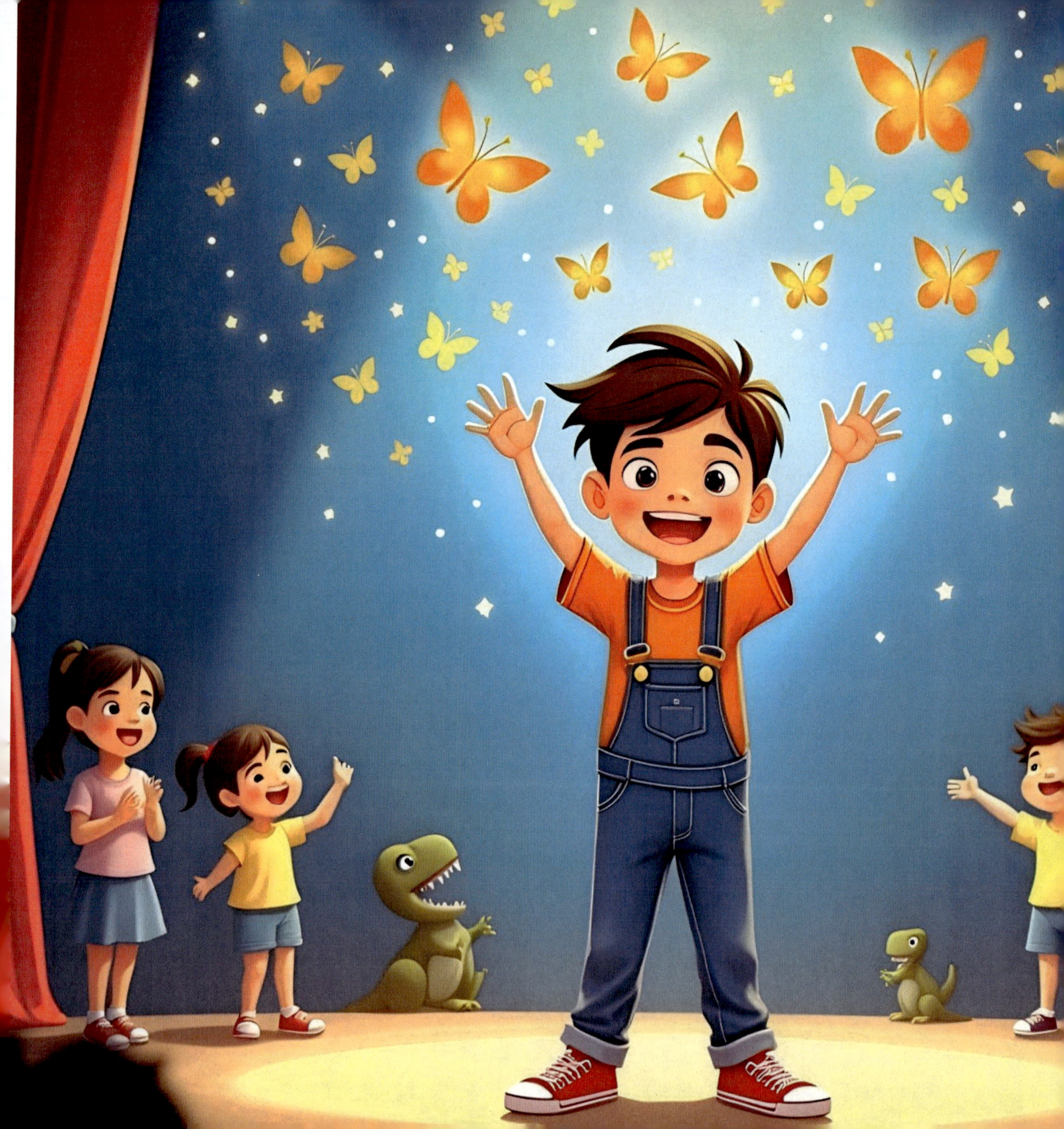

Everyone claps after Theo's song! "The **butterflies** helped me be brave!" says Theo. "They weren't scary - they helped me **shine**!"

Creative Notes

The Little Book of

As a way of saying thank you.
I am thrilled to gift you this FREE coloring book.

To get instant access just scan QR code or go to:

www.booksbyluna.com

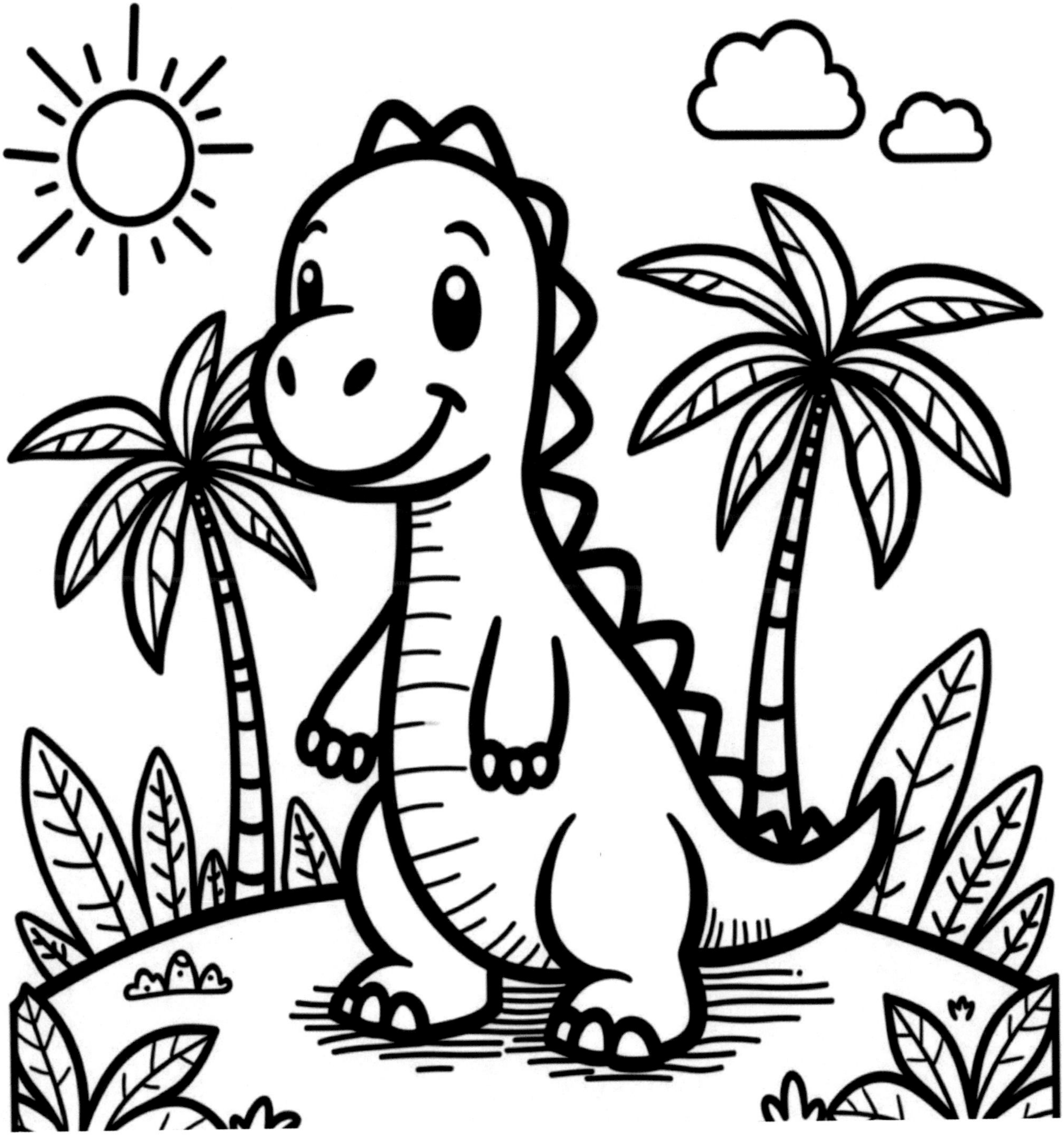

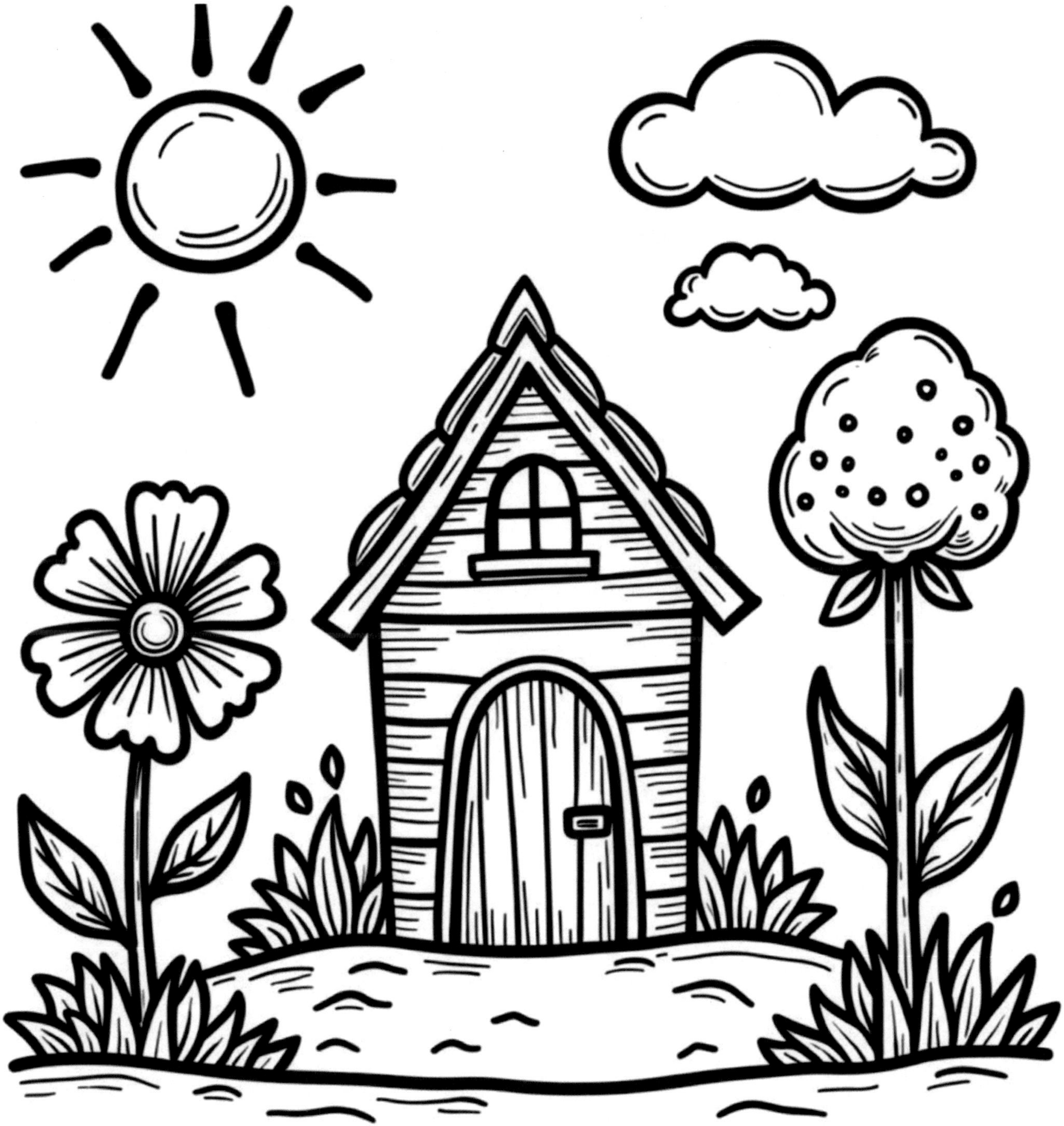

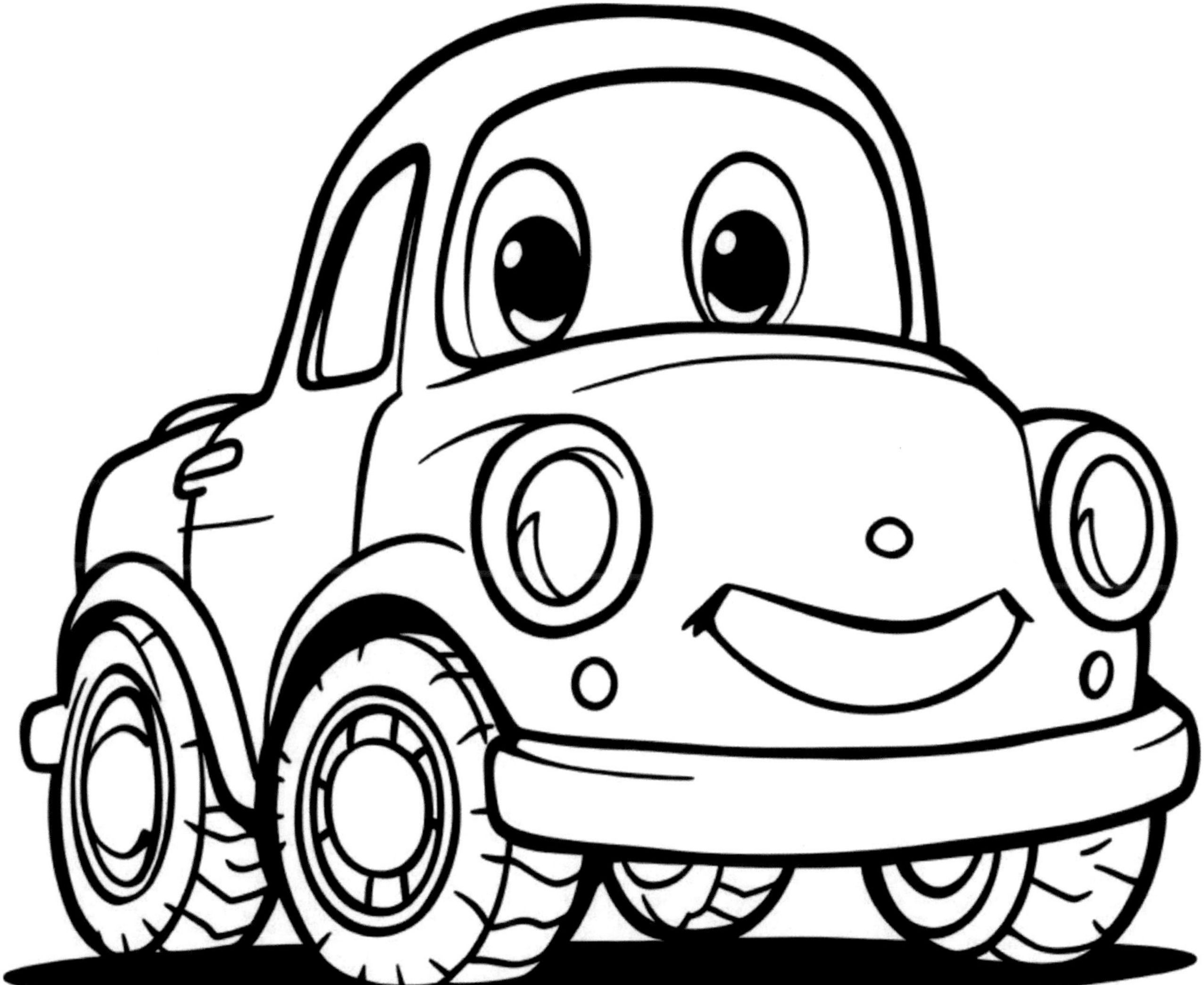

Made in the USA
Middletown, DE
01 March 2025